FIVE LOSE
DAD IN THE
GARDEN CENTRE

Other adventures in this series:

Enid Blyton®

FIVE LOSE DAD IN THE GARDEN CENTRE

Text by
Bruno Vincent

Enid Blyton for Grown-Ups

Quercus

First published in Great Britain in 2017 by

Quercus Editions Ltd
Carmelite House
50 Victoria Embankment
London EC4Y 0DZ

An Hachette UK company

A CIP catalogue record for this book is available
from the British Library

ISBN 978 1 78648 755 1

Text by Bruno Vincent
Original illustrations by Eileen A. Soper
Cover illustration by Ruth Palmer

10 9 8 7 6 5 4 3 2 1

Typeset by CC Book Production

Printed and bound in Germany by GGP Media GmbH

Contents

CHAPTER ONE

An Unexpected Visit

It was a beautiful summer's day in Dorset. The sun was high and hot in the clear sky, making holidaymakers reach gratefully for their hats, dark glasses and sunscreen. Over the clifftop where Kirrin Cottage was located, though, a keen wind whipped away the worst of the heat, leaving only the glorious benefits of sunshine.

'Oh, darling!' came Aunt Fanny's voice. 'Look who's here!'

Uncle Quentin nearly fell off his stool. Unexpected visitors to Kirrin Cottage – at least ones he was supposed to talk to – were unheard of. He had seen to this by making sure that anyone who came to the door expecting a cheery greeting left under no illusion that they were anything but a monstrous interruption to his routine. He huffed and sighed and looked at his watch until visitors were provoked beyond endurance and beat

1

their retreat, delivering apologies that he mercilessly ignored.

So it had been these many years past. And so would it be now!

What made Quentin's heart lurch, however, was the possibility of Fanny coming into his office (against strictest instructions) to find him not there. To find, in fact, the doors of the dusty old wardrobe in the corner open and the old coats thrust aside, disclosing a ladder which passed into a shaft in the floor. A shaft up which shone the bright lights of a top-class modern laboratory, and from which also drifted a few wisps of sweet-smelling pipe smoke.

Then the questions would begin. Begin? They might never stop.

'Quentin?' called Aunt Fanny again. 'Are you in there? Oh, he's fallen asleep again . . .'

Her voice was relayed through a PA, high on the laboratory wall, from the microphone he had secreted outside his office door.

Quentin switched off the oxyacetylene torch he had been using and placed it back in its holder, then threw his pipe on to the nearest surface and rushed to the hatch. No

'Oh, darling!' came Aunt Fanny's voice.
'Looks who's here!'

time to use the motorized ladder lift of his own invention – elegant and comfortable, perhaps, but much too slow. He pulled himself up rung over rung until he lurched into the office, slammed the doors of the wardrobe shut and leant against them, panting.

'Quentin!' Fanny said insistently. 'I'm coming in!'

He saw the door handle start to turn, and checked himself over. He brushed some steel fibres off his chest, took a deep gulp of air to try and regulate his breathing, and popped a mint in his mouth. At the last moment, as the door came open, he suddenly remembered the plastic goggles he was wearing, and whipped them off with a gasp of terror, stuffing them down the back of his waistband.

'*There* you are,' Fanny said. 'Didn't you hear me calling?'

'Oh, er, did I? I'm not sure,' Quentin said, assuming the air of scholarly abstraction that he generally wore to get away with not paying attention. He plumped himself down into his leather chair and then stiffened with discomfort as the goggles stuck into his lower back.

'Sorry,' he said. 'I was, er . . .' He waved at his desk vaguely, presuming that this gesture alone vouchsafed that he had been hard at work. The only paperwork there was a copy of the *Racing Post*.

'Yes,' Fanny said, peering over her reading glasses, 'I can see you've been hard at it.'

The dotting around of evidence that Quentin was in fact a bored retiree pretending to work was one of his meanest (and cleverest) tricks: a deception about which he at least had the decency to feel a modicum of guilt. It worked because it gave Fanny the sense that she knew what was *really* going on.

'Come on,' she said peremptorily. 'Don't sit down. Get up. They're here.'

Quentin was too distracted by his recent narrow escape to put up a protest, or ask who. Instead, he rose and somewhat meekly followed Fanny out, massaging his back.

'We'll have to get you a more egocentric chair,' said Fanny, noticing this, as they went through the kitchen to the front door.

He turned to her, his meekness at once forgotten, as she had touched upon an ever-sensitive subject.

'Don't start on about clearing my office out again,' he

*There was a tense stand-off that had so far
lasted several days.*

barked. 'Just don't. Everything's fine as it is. I don't want anybody messing—'

'Oh yes, I know, I know,' said Aunt Fanny, reaching for the front door. 'Let's not fight before receiving visitors.'

'Besides, it's *ergonomic*,' he growled.

As Fanny opened the front door and cried out her welcomes, Quentin couldn't help his mood (which had been quite buoyant) sliding back to its accustomed grumpiness.

The renovation of his office had been a long-term ambition of his wife's, and was the sorest of sore points between them. He knew that she was desperate to do it because she objected to the room's (as she put it) 'ingrained loathsomeness', and that his refusal to have it cleaned presented a myriad of threats to the health of the rest of the house – among them rot, damp, infestation and general malodorousness. She also pointed out that, if they did not have it looked at soon, it could seriously deplete the value of the house if they ever moved – a prospect which made him snort with derision. (A response which itself did not improve the tone of the conversation.)

However, the room could not be renovated – or even properly looked over by an architect – without the discovery of the secret he had kept from her for so long. But her desire for the office's (as George had put it) 'de-crappening' never wavered or weakened. And he knew it never would.

It was an insoluble problem. So, despite the fact that he was an inventor and solved problems for a living, the only course Quentin had come up with was to fight back implacably with all his strength.

He could, at times, be a tad stubborn.

So, depressed at this fresh recommencement of the eternal battle, Quentin shuffled outside morosely to see who the devil this could be, infesting his afternoon with their presence. And, at the same moment, he made up his mind to amuse himself by attaining new levels of beastliness.

He saw a car with four young people getting out of it, one of them hugging Fanny, and then he saw a brown blur streaking in his direction and found Timmy leaping up and licking his face.

Seeing him, the car's inhabitants all waved cheerily.

'Oh,' he said. 'It's you lot.'

CHAPTER TWO

A Dastardly Plan Comes to Fruition

'Okay, yes, thank you. That's enough of that,' he said. Quentin stepped back so the dog went on all fours, and then patted its head. He had never accustomed himself to overt displays of emotion, and with his sixty-fifth birthday on the horizon, he wasn't likely to change now.

'Daddy!' said George, giving him a big hug.

'Okay, yes, thank you,' he said, waiting until she stopped. Restraining himself from giving her a pat on the head, he instead offered a businesslike smile – a brief compression of the lips. 'It's nice to see you,' he said.

'You too, you rummy old codger,' she said. 'God, you stink of tobacco. How Mummy doesn't notice it is beyond me. Come on, Timmy; let's go inside, away from stinky Grandpa!'

Loathing declarations of love as he did, Quentin found

George's insults much more his cup of tea, and as he watched her run inside with her beloved dog, he started to feel something like parental benevolence.

It was, however, a feeling that quickly soured.

'Unkie Q!' came a jocular voice. Quentin suppressed an urge to grimace. There was something about Julian's bonhomie that was so false and jarring it gave Quentin a pain behind the eyes. What didn't help was that Quentin's evident distaste made the young man try ever harder to win him round, meaning they were locked in a vicious circle.

As Julian bounded over, Quentin forced an expression which was a smile in name alone. However, the young man was holding something bottle shaped, which he seemed to be proffering.

'What are you doing here?' asked Aunt Fanny, as George reappeared out of the house, to fetch luggage.

'Felt like a getaway,' said George. 'Sorry I didn't phone.'

'We're not at all ready for you,' said Fanny. 'I'll, er, have to check ... It's *so* nice to see you, darling,' she said, giving George another hug. They had recently made up after a dreadful misunderstanding over the correct date

10

of Mothering Sunday, and relations between them were better than they had been for years.

'Actually, we were thinking of staying in a hotel in Bridport for a night, then maybe pushing on into Devon tomorrow.'

'Bit tarty, Bridport, if you ask me,' Quentin said stiffly. 'Not real Dorset.'

'Quite right,' said Fanny. 'And you'll do no such thing. You can stay here; just give me fifteen minutes to check the . . . er, to find the things. Check the cupboards.' Fanny seemed suddenly to grow nervous and self-conscious. Quentin saw a meaningful look pass between her and George, followed by them both darting a nervous glance towards him.

Before he could think about it, however, Julian held the bottle up closer to his face for him to inspect. 'Port,' he said.

'For me?' he asked.

'Yup!' Julian said.

'Why?'

'It's a Father's Day present for next week,' said Julian. 'In advance, because I know George isn't going to buy you anything. She said so. "Commercialized horse doings", she called it. Except she didn't use the word "doings", of course. So, when I saw this, I thought of you. Just, ah, cushioning the blow.'

'Oh, I don't care about that,' said Quentin. 'Forgetting Father's Day is a family tradition. I did it, and so did my father before me. Still, this is jolly nice of you.' Quentin felt rather awkward, about the disparaging thoughts he had lately entertained towards Julian, as those feelings receded in the distance. Perhaps he was a decent sort of cove, deep down . . .

'Oh, Quentin's got to go there,' Fanny was saying to George. 'Haven't you, Q?'

'What?' he asked.

'They're going antique hunting – next door to the optician's in Dorchester.'

'Oh, must I?' he asked grumpily. 'I thought you were going to do it.'

'You know you must. Also, I can't be fetching everything for you all the time,' said Fanny with unwonted steel in her voice. 'If I keeled over tomorrow, where would you be then? You must learn a measure of independence.'

Anyone who came to the door expecting a cheery greeting left under no illusion that they were a monstrous interruption to his routine.

'We can go for oysters afterwards at the fish bar over the road,' said Dick. 'They've got a special offer on. My treat.'

Oysters, thought Quentin. He hadn't had oysters in the longest time. He could never resist them.

'Well,' he said, looking at the bottle in his hand. 'Why not, after all?'

Within moments, they were back in the car (now relieved of its luggage), and three-point-turning to go back down the road towards the mainland proper.

'Nice of you to give me a lift,' said Quentin.

'Not at all,' said Julian over his shoulder, from the driver's seat.

Silence set in.

'I really can't turn down an oyster,' said Quentin. 'Never could.'

'Mmm,' said Dick distractedly. 'Me too.'

Quentin looked around the car. It was very odd to find himself being the chatterbox in a group. Usually, when he was with these youngsters, one could hardly get them to shut up. Especially when setting out on a jolly excursion like this. Yet now they seemed tense and thoughtful.

14

He looked at the bottle in his hand, which he had neglected to leave at the house. That was a most unusual gesture, as well.

Quentin looked around at the other passengers of the car again, and found them all looking forward. He began to feel quite uncomfortable.

As though he could sense Quentin's thoughts, Julian suddenly sped up. Quentin saw his fingers straying close to the button that locked the car doors.

He thought back to the nervousness with which Fanny had stumbled over her words, as though she had been sticking to an agreed script, followed by that conspiratorial look with George. It was almost as though . . . as though they had all been brainwashed . . .

He had the uneasy feeling that there was an organized plot going on. One minute he had been in his laboratory and the next he was in a car, on the way to Dorchester.

And suddenly, with sickening certainty, he saw what the plot was.

'STOP THE CAR!' he yelled.

Julian didn't slow, and in fact sped up again, but when Quentin shouted a second time, even louder, with Timmy now barking from the boot, Julian saw that continuing all the way to Dorchester was quite impossible. He braked to a slewing halt. Quentin jumped out, and started running back towards the house.

'No,' he was saying. 'Please, no . . .'

The house came back into view around the corner and he saw that he was right. Feelings of anger and helplessness swept over him.

Outside the house was a van, which must have been parked down on the beach while Quentin was being dispensed with. On the side, in bright letters, was painted the name of a local building firm.

Seeing him coming towards the house, Fanny came up the road to try to stop him. The builders, two sturdy, shaven-headed men, followed her. As she reached him, Quentin bent over, panting.

'Now,' she said. 'I'm sorry I had to resort to this. But, you see, to get a builder round in business hours to look at the place in daylight, and give a quote, I had to get you out of here. And you knew this had to happen sooner or later . . . Quentin? What's wrong?'

As he straightened, she saw that her husband had gone

pale, and a look of terror spread across his face. During his brief sprint along the gravel road, Quentin had been preparing a bombastic speech about this outrageous behaviour. How it was a breach of trust, an invasion of privacy. And a gross betrayal of something or other.

But the words faded from his lips. For he had suddenly remembered where, in his distraction, he had put down his pipe. He had sent it skittering over the desk, where it had come to rest in a pile of scrunched-up papers, which it was sure to have set alight. These were on top of a pad and beside a large stack of further papers. The table on which these sat was wooden. And, beneath it, was the kerosene can which powered the house's emergency backup generator. Next to which was the pure oxygen cylinder for the oxyacetylene torch.

'I think we should all duck,' said Quentin, crouching and holding his hands over his head.

Well, he's lost it at last, thought Fanny. I suppose I'm surprised he lasted this long. She was turning to apologize to the builders for her husband's eccentric behaviour when the ground under their feet trembled. This was followed by the sound of a loud, deep thump from within the house.

Fanny had always been a woman who took things in her stride.
'Well, gentlemen,' she said, turning to the builders.
'It seems your visit is well timed.'

They all ducked, then turned to look. As they did so, the far back corner of the house quivered and fell in.

Fanny had always been a woman who took things in her stride.

'Well, gentlemen,' she said, turning to the builders. 'It seems your visit is well timed.'

CHAPTER THREE

In the Doghouse

George admired the skill and audacity of Fanny's plan. The fact that it hadn't entirely worked was not at all down to a failure of planning, but a combination of poor luck, bad acting and Quentin's tenacious paranoia.

But Quentin was not the only stubborn old guy in George's life. In dog years, Timmy was far older than Quentin. In some ways, he could be even more stubborn. (They both frequently ponged a bit too – in fact, there were more similarities than George was entirely comfortable with, so she chose not to pursue this line of thought.)

It was Timmy's basket that had recently become an issue within the house. They all loved Timmy as much as they ever had, but the foam basket in which he spent his nights and most of his days was starting to smell so badly it was putting them off their meals. Or, rather, it was forcing them to eat their meals sitting on the sofa – increasing the danger of spillages, which concerned Anne so much she was becoming a bore on the subject.

George agreed. The basket had to go. But how to replace it?

'He's really attached to that thing,' she said.

'Well, he's in it about twenty-three hours a day,' said Julian. 'I'm surprised it's not fused to his skin.'

'It's such a peculiarly awful stench,' said Anne. 'It's like a combination of about six different unpleasant things. Sweat, and spit, and . . . well, the mind boggles, really . . .'

'All right,' said George. 'Let's leave him his dignity. I've agreed the basket should be changed. But how? Do you remember last time?'

A silence fell around the table. They did indeed remember. Several years ago, George had innocently thrown away Timmy's current basket, assuming he would be pleased with his nice new one – a rather upmarket affair, sturdy and made of wicker, with a washable woollen lining. He loathed it on sight, however, and growled when forced to come within six feet of it. The next morning, George found the new basket had been the subject of a dirty protest, with no Timmy to be seen.

A panicky search followed, and eventually they discovered him at the back of the flats, happily asleep in his own, trash-besmeared basket, which with infinite resourcefulness he had somehow rescued from the dustbin.

George had been forced to give Timmy a bath to get the smell of coffee grounds and mouldy bananas off him. It was not an experience that either of them had enjoyed.

A few months later, when she thought he had forgotten about it, George tried again to remove his basket, but without success.

'I think the key is,' she said, utilizing the devious-to-be-kind thought processes of a parent, 'to go on the charm offensive. We need to win him over to a new basket to make him forget the old one.'

'To the pet store, then,' said Dick.

'"Pet shop", Dick,' said Julian. 'We are not in Nebraska.'

'To neither,' George said. 'There's no pet shop I'm aware of anywhere near here that has a wide enough selection.'

'Where should we go, then?'

'Well, I've been thinking,' George said. 'About the situation at Kirrin Cottage . . .'

*

'To the pet store, then,' said Dick.
'"Pet shop", Dick,' said Julian. 'We are not in Nebraska.'

The situation at Kirrin Cottage was far from ideal.

There was a tense stand-off that had so far lasted several days. Aunt Fanny's position was entirely straight-forward: that Quentin had been systematically lying to her for years, and that he had also blown up a quarter of their house, in circumstances that were not covered by insurance.

Quentin, on the other hand, held that, if his wife had not interrupted him with her foolish roundabout scheme to get him out of the house, none of this would have happened at all. In this, he was technically correct, and, taking the high ground on this issue, he chose not to dignify the other charges (in which he was demonstrably in the wrong) with a response.

So, a stand-off prevailed – one which, as it approached a week's duration, was in dire need of a mediator.

Just such a figure appeared one night in the unlikely person of Julian. He had heard George's plan and agreed it was sound. Thus he phoned first Fanny, then Quentin, and a deal was struck.

It was agreed that Quentin would have a replacement laboratory. But, as happens sooner or later to all married

24

men with weird and disagreeable hobbies, henceforward he was to be forced to practise it in a shed, or not at all. This naturally precipitated the purchasing of the aforementioned shed, which would be a further expense. But there was plenty of room for it in the grounds of the cottage, and (Fanny conceded) at least then, if he blew himself up with one of his beastly contraptions, he wouldn't take the rest of the house with him.

Now, at last, they could move forward. Fanny could look towards having the whole of the house to herself (and returning Quentin's former office to a drawing room, with an open fire), while Quentin could get excited about the type of shed he wanted.

After some brief research it was clear that there was only one place in the south-west to go for such a shed. This was Garden Universe, an enormous, sprawling garden centre in the countryside, cleverly placed to be equidistant from three medium-sized cities.

Garden Universe catered to people's need for garden plants, to be sure – but that was really just one tiny green shoot of the vast underground root network. It boasted an astonishing array of other items, including, as well as sheds, and, importantly for George, 'Europe's widest selection of pet-related products'.

Thus it was that, a few days later, the four housemates, Timmy and Quentin all found themselves in the same car, slowing down to turn into Garden Universe's car park.

'You see,' said George. 'I told you we'd gone too far.'

'Oh shut up, George,' said Julian. 'No one likes a smug git.'

Maybe that's why no one likes you, then, fatso, she thought, but instead of saying anything, she just fixed him with a placid smile.

Anne, squashed in the middle of the back seat, would normally have been the person to break them up and tell them both to be a bit more grown-up. But her attention was entirely distracted by being next to Quentin. For some reason or other, she had never been very close to him before, except for the reluctant semi-annual peck on the cheek. The experience was quite alarming.

Although he seemed, from a distance, to be rather a modest-sized man, next to her in the car he seemed to tower over Anne, bulging in all sorts of unexpected areas and with thickets of hair sprouting from alarming places.

Also, there was the curious odour Anne occasionally got hints of, which was not entirely *un*pleasant, but (if one were to be strictly honest) not particularly pleasant either. It was reminiscent of a too briefly shampooed pub carpet – one got a sense of a surface cleanliness struggling to mask a more lasting and ingrained squalor. Anne kept trying discreetly to squinch across the seat away from him and closer to Dick, but each time Quentin's bulk expanded to fill the space she had created.

She was happy to be distracted from these contemplations by the louder than usual argument between Julian and George in the front seat, over where to park.

'Just park anywhere, you buffoon; it doesn't matter!' George was saying.

'But just hang on. Do we want to be closer to the exit, for speed of egress,' Julian asked, 'or closer to the entrance, in case we have to carry stuff?'

Having set off in good time, they had most definitely beaten the rush, if rush there was likely to be on a Tuesday morning in term time, and were presented with about three hundred acres of car parking spaces dotted with occasional vehicles.

'God, there's even a Rainforest Zone,' said Dick.
'It's like being in the bloody Crystal Maze.'

'I'm going to go mad if you don't just park somewhere,' George said.

'Fine, fine,' said Julian, still dithering.

'Life is short,' George said. She was about to add, 'Or yours will be, anyway, if you don't bloody park in the next forty secs,' but was cut short by being thrown forward in her seat as the car braked sharply.

'Here we are,' said Julian. 'Aren't we, folks?'

'Woof!' said Timmy.

Struggling to catch her breath after being winded by her seat belt, Anne was startled to find that both Dick and Quentin, either side of her, were fast asleep.

CHAPTER FOUR

Garden Universe

Once out of the car, they began to walk towards the main building. Julian and George were somewhat tired from bickering and, aware that they were only at the beginning of what promised to be a very long day, had decided to calm it down for the time being. (At least, that was what they told themselves. The fact was that they both thoroughly enjoyed bickering and, refreshed from the recent bout, were, for the time being, replete.)

Knowing the reputation of the place as a gargantuan retail megalith, Dick had expected the main building to loom enormously above them in the manner of an American hypermarket. But in fact it did not interrupt the skyline at all, instead extending out into the distance in a pattern of one-storey peaked roofs, as though to give the impression it was made up of hundreds of greenhouses that huddled together out of a sense of community spirit.

Outside the entrance, George took commission of an enormous trolley, which Timmy at once jumped into, with an excited woof.

'Lazy beast,' she said, as he curled up to sleep. Then she saw her father looking at Timmy jealously. 'Not you too,' she said, steering it away from him. 'You have to walk.'

The first thing they came to was a large sign giving a layout of the grounds of the entire complex. It stood six feet across and nine feet tall. They gawped at it for a few moments uncomprehendingly, until George had the presence of mind to take a photo on her phone for future reference.

'God, there's even a Rainforest Zone,' said Dick. 'It's like being in the bloody Crystal Maze.'

'Okay,' said Anne. 'Well, let's not get too befuddled by this map. It's rather a lot to take in. We're obviously going to be here all day, so, first thing, why don't we just have a bit of a wander. And stop at eleven for a coffee. After that, we get the shed for Uncle Quentin, and, for our canine friend, a B.A.S.K.E.T.'

Julian chuckled. 'You don't need to spell out "basket", Anne; it's not like he can un—'

He was cut off by the way in which, at the word 'basket', Timmy leapt to his feet, turned towards Julian whip-smart, and trained upon him a keen, unflinching gaze. The others were all looking at Julian like he was a lunatic. He chuckled nervously. 'I, uh, I mean,' he said, improvising fiercely, 'I mean, no *biscuit*. No biscuit for me. Ha ha! No, sir. On a diet.' He patted his stomach. 'No biscuit with my coffee. I don't even like biscuits, really . . .'

Timmy was reluctantly persuaded by this to relax the vigilance of his stare, and although he curled back into a comfortable circle, his head resting on his paws, his eyes still turned every few seconds to give Julian a cool stare.

Free to roam, they all began to drift somewhat aimlessly through the departments.

They were quickly reduced to a sort of dreamy peacefulness. The garden centre didn't seem to cater to *rich* customers, exactly, but it offered such a wide range of upmarket lines and products that walking through it gave one a vaguely pleasant ache of aspiration.

'Funny, isn't it,' said Julian, watching people drift past.

'What is?' asked George.

'Come on, Timmy, let's go inside,
away from stinky Grandpa!'

'People seem to come here just to drift around and not buy stuff.'

'They're probably lost,' said George. 'I know I am. Where's Quentin got to? Oh, there he is, trying on a hat.'

The last time any of them had been in a garden centre, they had been dragged round by their parents. In those days, the name denoted a football-pitch-sized plot filled with potted plants, urns and statuary, with a building at one end for the checkout and packets of seeds.

Now, as they meandered through the aisles, the four of them saw what was on sale with ever-replenishing astonishment. That a so-called garden centre would stock fine china seemed absurd at first. But this was quickly forgotten once they came open the section boasting the in-house bakery, organic butcher's and delicatessen – which was next to the children's book section.

Dick promised himself he would not make any rash or foolish purchases, so came away with some Moroccan spiced almonds, a Russian doll depicting the last six England football managers and a book entitled *Teach Yourself Flamenco Guitar*. (Dick did not own a guitar.) Julian, meanwhile, availed himself of a brace of frozen quail.

'Or are they woodcocks, would you say?' Julian wondered, holding them up as they exited the deli. 'Look, you can still see the shotgun pell—*don't move*!' Dick froze, and, using him as a shield while looking over his shoulder, Julian followed the progress of someone walking lazily past.

'It's that girl from uni,' he said. 'Emily whatsername.'

Dick essayed a look over his shoulder, to check Julian was correct. He knew the girl, remembering how Julian had mooned helplessly after her. On one occasion, Julian had done so in both senses, after he had got angrily drunk on port over lunch in the student bar, and spotted her in the courtyard outside. But she had never seemed to notice him.

'I could have gone out with her,' Julian said bitterly. 'If only I'd had the guts to ask.'

Dick knew full well that this was not the case, but decided to keep the intelligence to himself and allow the fantasy to fizzle out of its own accord.

'Look at that guy she's holding hands with,' Julian muttered. 'What a drip. I bet *he* didn't get a double first from Cambridge.'

'Neither did you,' said George. She was looking around,

vexed. 'Where the bloody hell *is* Quentin? Oh, there. Trying out a golf club.'

'Just look at that fake contentment,' Julian whispered. 'I've never seen people trying so hard to look happy. It's pathetic. What are they hiding? Don't you agree, Dick?'

Dick thought that the couple in question were drifting through life exuding, quite convincingly, the bliss of new love. But he chose not to say so, and instead busied himself with a shelf of Burt Lancaster westerns on DVD.

'Is there anything that they don't sell, do you think?' he asked. 'We could run a book on it, see who finds the unlikeliest item. I'll go first: pony gas masks.'

Julian had been skulking along, looking like the entire world was out to ruin his day, and muttering about good-looking girls going out with 'preppy milque toasts'. But, at Dick's suggestion, he perked up.

'Okay, I'll go. Sashimi,' he said.

'Good one,' Dick said. He thought about his next answer. 'Birth control,' he said.

'What type?' Julian asked.

'Pill.'

36

'This feels good,' said Julian. 'To be tracking the bugger. We've got him in our sights. Like a noble deer on the mountain.'
'Oh do shut up, Julian.'

Julian nodded. 'Okay, my next one: gluten-free dog treats.'

Dick laughed. They turned a corner, and Julian grabbed his wrist. 'Keep going,' he muttered.

'What, to the car accessories section?' Dick asked.

'Anywhere,' said Julian. 'Look. That's Driscoll the Destroyer!'

'Oh, cripes,' said Dick. They dashed into a nearby aisle and peeped around the corner. Neither had any intention of being spotted by Dennis Driscoll. He had been the terror of the local rugby team when they were growing up. He was a mountain of a man, imperious, confident, handsome, and more than somewhat a bully.

Nothing good could come from saying hello to him. He would recall stories of their weakness and ineptitude at high volume, and then deafen them with his laughter, clearly expecting Dick and Julian to join in. No matter what they tried, the conversation would tilt towards how much better his life was than theirs. He was, as even Dick, the inveterate diplomat, admitted, 'a bit of a pain'.

'Has he seen us?' Dick asked.

'No. And look! He's changed! He looks like shit!'

Dick peeked out. It was true. Gone was the burly smiling boulder of yesteryear, and in his place was a rather hollow-eyed, meek sort of chap. His physique, which had formerly been large around the shoulders and narrow around the waist, was now the other way round.

'Please put your feet back in the buggy for Daddy,' he was saying to his little girl, who was both kicking and screaming.

'Here, you dropped this,' he said, picking up the rattly toy she had thrown out of the pushchair. The child, who was invisible to Dick and Julian, immediately threw the toy on to the ground again. Driscoll bent and picked it up.

'Try not to do that again, darling,' he said patiently, handing it back to her. 'You'll get it dirty.' It was immediately thrown out again. Driscoll looked down at it and sighed.

'Please, darling . . .' he said gently.

'Bravo, that child! Encore!' whispered Julian.

'Well, that's certainly a turnaround,' said Dick, as Driscoll the Destroyer wearily pushed his pram away.

'Did you see the puke stains on his shirt?' Julian asked, victorious. 'Ha!'

Dick and Julian set off in the opposite direction with a spring in their step. Julian was feeling positively jaunty. He checked the time on his phone.

'Nearly time for a pint, I would have thought . . .' he said.

'Oh, Julian,' said Dick. 'Not before eleven, surely. Besides, they won't serve beer here, will they?'

In response, Julian merely pointed over Dick's shoulder. With a sad sense of inevitability, the younger brother turned to find himself standing outside the entrance to *Diarmuid O'MacCaughrean's Irish Patio Bar – fully licensed*. Dick shuddered as Julian opened the door, bracing himself for an onslaught of plastic Celtic crosses, replica Blarney stones and the like.

'Where the effing eff,' said George, wandering into the spot where they had just stood, and self-censoring her language owing to the children within earshot, 'is my selfish . . .' – she struggled for a moment to find the right word – '*eff*ing father?'

Anne looked up from trying on some sunglasses, and shrugged.

'Woof,' said Timmy, mystified.

CHAPTER FIVE

Parental Neglect

George and Anne reclaimed Dick and Julian from the Irish pub in time for them to meet Uncle Quentin at the café, where they found him peacefully pouring tea from a pot.

'There you are,' said George. 'Where did you get to?'

Quentin gave a minuscule sort of semi-shrug, and attended himself to his tea.

'Well, you're here, at least,' said Anne. Quentin studied the newspaper in front of him.

The boys sat down with a thump, having tarried at the counter to order the group's coffees, cakes and water bowl.

'This place is incredible,' said Julian.

'I still can't quite tell where we are on this map,' said George, peering at her phone and expanding the image, then swiping to explore it. 'I think we're in the Inigo Jones Tea Room,' she said, looking around. 'Wait a minute – where's Daddy?'

They all looked at Quentin's chair. Astoundingly, it was empty.

'How did he do that?' asked Anne.

Dick and Julian were sent to hunt him down. They returned shortly with Quentin in tow.

'Where did you go?' George asked.

Quentin merely sat, taking the newspaper out from under his arm. At first, everyone assumed he was just being stubborn, as usual. But then they wondered whether he had heard her at all – or even if his attention was wandering.

'I wish you wouldn't disappear like that,' said George. 'We've got to get the shed business sorted out this afternoon. Now, I was thinking, if we split up and have a preliminary look at them before lunch, we can meet up and . . . Where's he got to *now*?'

George had turned her head, mid-sentence, to include the others in her plans, and as she looked back to Quentin to see if he understood anything of what she was saying, was stunned to be presented with an empty chair yet again.

The group saw him over at the counter, perusing the cheesecakes. It was the work of a further minute to get him back and sat down.

42

'There's abstracted thought,' George said, 'and plain brainlessness. How can we tell which one is which? What is Daddy thinking about when he goes like that?'

'Quentin, you're impossible!' said Anne, as he took up his newspaper again.

'Really, Uncle,' said Dick, 'I think you could pay attention for at least a minute.'

'Of course, of course,' Quentin said. Then, seeing this was not quite sufficient to placate them, he added, 'I'm very grateful for you bringing me here.' He set down his newspaper, not knowing that George had been on the verge of snatching it from him, hitting him smartly across the forehead with it, and ripping it in half. Deprived of this satisfaction, she merely fixed him with a simmering stare.

George then reiterated her plan, and all agreed upon it, just in time for their elevenses to arrive on a tray. Conversation returned to how amazing this place was and what a needlessly profuse shopping experience it provided, while blood-sugar levels rose all round, returning them to a more equable mood.

It was with amused consternation, then, rather than the expected raw fury, that they noticed some fifteen minutes later that Quentin had absented himself once more.

Julian and Dick hunted in one direction while George

and Timmy went in another, both teams returning to the table (where Anne was holding the fort) empty-handed.

'What's his game?' asked Dick.

George sat down and shook her head. 'I don't know. It's very hard to tell. He prefers not to be understood, if possible. I sometimes wonder if he has any feelings at all.'

'Oh, George, that's not very nice,' said Anne.

But the boys weren't entirely on Anne's side.

'Didn't you notice, Anne,' Julian pointed out, 'that he refused to talk to either you or George? He only replied to Dick. Is that usual, George?'

Julian had hit upon a sore point, which George ignored in familial fashion. The others returned to the crumbs of their cakes.

They refused to believe that Quentin would remain missing for any serious length of time. In fact, they were content to let him roam and amuse himself for now, so they could then hopefully get him to focus on sheds when they needed him to, later on. In the meantime, they assumed they would catch sight of him every once in a while, wandering between departments.

With this in mind, they settled to enjoy their coffee. However, conversation soon ran dry, and they found themselves looking around with mild concern.

'Is Quentin feeling quite all right, do you think?' Julian asked.

George opened her mouth to say yes, of course. And hesitated. There was an uneasy moment's silence at the table.

'I think so,' she said.

Anne looked pained. 'I'm sure he's fine,' she said, in her usual pert, conciliatory voice. But, in fact, she was far from reassured. This doubt over, and fear for, their parents' health, was quite a new thing in their lives – but one they were trying to get used to, because they knew it was not going to go away.

'I do see him being a bit vacant sometimes,' George admitted quietly.

'But that's practically the MO of the genius scientist,' said Julian. 'They're always standing about the place and looking out of the window, having profound thoughts.'

George crinkled up her nose, unconvinced. 'When was the last time he produced a major invention, though?'

'There was that incubation tank, for the long-term storage of meat and vegetables. That was impressive.'

'Dick, he just fixed the freezer,' George said.

'Oh,' Dick said. 'That thing was already there? He didn't invent it?'

'*No*,' said George, tempted to add that it was not in her father's habit to stencil *INDESIT* on the front of his inventions.

'Still,' Anne said, 'he has to ruminate. It's ninety per cent of the job for an old clever clogs like him, I bet.'

'Yes, but there's abstracted thought,' George said, 'and plain brainlessness. How can we tell which one is which? What is he thinking about when he goes like that?'

George was never to discover what Quentin thought about when he went 'like that', but in fact when Quentin appeared dazed, he was usually thinking about was the next day's racing. He didn't merely use the *Racing Post* as a prop. He really did like to stick on a bet or two in the afternoon, and (having memorized the form sheet each morning) he spent his spare moments comparing the goings, track history, riders and so forth, at the day's meetings.

'When I find that old git,' said George, 'I'm going to wring his bloody neck.'

As a creative person, Quentin found that all his useful thoughts arrived of their own accord when he was engrossed in everyday tasks. All his best breakthroughs (or 'breaksthrough', as he would have it) occurred during or after he was performing his toilet, preparing tea, pottering about the house, writing emails, or thinking about what bets he would put on. Trying hard to think directly about a problem was, in fact, the one way he had found that was guaranteed *not* to get a result.

Therefore, as he pushed his trolley along, whistling happily to himself, Quentin was thinking about that afternoon's runners and riders at Sandown and Kempton Park, and quite sincerely considered himself to be working.

Suddenly, there was an unpleasant sensation in his chest. He reached up a hand to clutch at it.

CHAPTER SIX

Health Concerns

'He's not answering his phone,' said Anne.

They were all now getting rather concerned, but trying not to show it.

'Does he take medication?' Dick asked.

'Yes,' said George. 'Three kinds. But I don't know what they're for. They could just be vitamins and fish oil.'

'Hmm,' said Julian. 'Even I take those.'

'Let's look for him, anyway,' George said, determined to be cheerful, and not to worry unnecessarily. 'He's bound to be nearby. Where do you think he might have gone?'

They gathered round George's map. They saw that the tea room was surrounded by a gift section, which he would have no interest in, a bath oils and perfume department, which he would be entirely blind to, and a children's clothing area, which he would find actively distasteful.

'There,' said George, prodding the map. 'That's where he went. Not too far from here.'

'Clothes?' Julian asked, somewhat doubtfully. 'He's never seemed that interested in clothes, to me. Those trousers of his are twenty years old, if they're a day.'

'Look closer,' said George, expanding the map. 'Look at the concessions *within* the department.'

'Jaeger!' said Anne. 'How lovely!'

'Dress your age, Anne,' said George gently. 'There's time for Jaeger. No – Harris Tweed. Daddy loves all that stuff; he's got a strange affinity for it. It makes him feel like a John Buchan hero, striding through the heather on his Scottish estate.'

'Let's go, then,' said Dick.

'Tally ho!' said Julian.

The five were somewhat out of practice when it came to tracking miscreants across alien terrain. Therefore, there was a fair amount of bickering, much consultation of the map and far too much lost time before they found themselves in the adult clothing section.

'This feels good,' said Julian. 'To be tracking the bugger.

We've got him in our sights. Like a noble deer on the mountain. Not knowing its days are numbered, that we're drawing a bead on its antlers—'

'Oh, do shut up, Julian,' said Anne. 'We'd be tracking him a lot closer if you hadn't stopped for a few pints.'

'We were looking at the map directly outside the bar,' Julian said, 'and we were getting in the way of pedestrians. It was mere politeness.'

'Still,' said Dick, 'I think we're on the right track. Look over there.'

The others stared, impressed that Dick had spotted a clue, but unsure what they were looking for. Dick walked up to the rather worried-looking lady on the Moss Bros stall, and engaged her in conversation.

'Yes,' she was telling Dick, as the others caught up with him. 'I was just telling my colleague, here. It was scary . . .'

'What was?' asked George.

'Well, there was this older gentleman, just like you describe,' the woman said (although she politely omitted to repeat Dick's description), 'walking through here, and, just by the door, there, he suddenly clutched his chest.'

There was a gasp of horror among the group.

'Didn't you do anything?' Anne asked.

'Of course,' said the woman. 'I rushed forward to see if he was okay, but he just waved me away, like I was being annoying, and said he was fine. Then he hurried on, out of the door.'

'Did you tell anyone?' Julian asked.

'Yes! I told my manager, Mr Wharton, that I thought this man was having a heart attack, and he just told me I was talking rubbish. He said no one who's having a heart attack is in a position to say they're all right. But I wasn't so convinced.'

The five said thanks (and woof) to the lady and made their way in the direction she pointed, as fast as they could. They found themselves at the aquarium section, a placid, mellow place, blanketed in soft blue light, where ripples played across the walls and ceiling.

'Through here,' said George, pressing on.

'Dick, *don't* stop to look at the tropical fish, for Pete's sake,' Anne said.

'But they're so beautiful,' Dick said quietly, before being yanked away by the hem of his jumper.

'But I didn't think there were any men like that anymore,'
Julian said, aghast.
'That's because you're not a woman,' George said.
'They're everywhere, mate.'

Around the next corner, they found themselves emerging into the light of day, and the garden furniture section. They were faced with a startling array of umbrellas, benches, ornaments, statuary, chairs, recliners, standing swings and objects whose utility was (to the four) a matter of pure speculation. Idiosyncratic, tasteless or ethereal as these items might be, they were organized with extreme strictness into ranks, rows and columns that spread out in every direction.

'Oh my *God*!' screamed George.

The very breath stopped in her cousins' throats. Far ahead of them, a pair of feet, apparently belonging to a man, stuck out from behind a garden bench. Some people were gathered nearby, looking worried, and as they ran closer they could see a young man performing CPR.

'Daddy!' cried George. 'Daddy! Are you . . . ? OH!' This final syllable was delivered at something of a squeak, which made Timmy (following on behind) jump, and then spin in a circle.

George found herself gazing down over what looked to be a training exercise. The body being operated upon was dressed in human clothes, but it had a head made of

55

white plastic: bald, expressionless, and staring at the sky with its mouth open.

Relief, embarrassment and shame flooded her in equal proportions, and George turned away, to be accepted by Anne's arms in a reassuring hug.

'I'm so sorry,' said Julian, catching up. 'Big misunder-standing. We've lost our dad – or our uncle . . .' He trailed off as the medic, without so much as batting an eyelid, and offering no more expression than the dummy he had been working on, turned away to have his face powdered by a make-up artist. Fifty feet away, Julian saw a very frustrated-looking man charging towards them.

'Filming *Doctors*,' said the young man who had been performing CPR; Julian realized now that he must be an actor, and the furious type getting closer by the second must be the director. 'They're doing a "found footage" episode,' the actor said.

'Budget cuts, eh?' Julian nodded sadly. 'Well, good luck. I hope you get to film back in the studio again soon.'

Spotting the incensed-looking bloke getting uncom-fortably close, Julian decided to cheese it in the opposite direction as fast as he could.

CHAPTER SEVEN

Desperate Measures

'It was just such a shock,' George said sorrowfully. 'So many awful things went through my head, all at once. And then, when I saw it wasn't him, I almost fainted.'

Anne, the group's nominated hugger, gave George an extra-hard squeeze, and stroked her back. 'I know it was horrible, darling,' she said.

'Glass of wine,' said Julian, putting one down next to her.

Looking around, Anne saw that they had wandered on to the Capability Brown Wine Terrace.

'She doesn't want *wine*, Julian,' Anne said to Julian testily. 'It's barely midday.'

'Actually, that would be good,' George said, picking up the glass and taking a hefty slurp. Naturally, Julian had not failed to order himself a glass too. Seeing them both tucking in made Dick feel that it was, on a holiday day, a perfectly acceptable hour to have a drink, so he went to order one himself. At which point, Anne, perceiving she was going to be the only abstainer, caught Dick's eye and mouthed the words, 'Go on, then.'

'Get a bottle; better value,' said Julian.

In a few minutes, they were all sitting at a table with glasses in front of them, Julian topping the others' glasses up, before adding twice as much to his own.

He plucked up a menu thinking it was a wine list, and perusing it, his eyebrows shot up. He looked round, and saw that the wine terrace was served by the adjacent food hall.

The owners of the garden centre did not lack in ambition when it came to the food on offer. There was a salad bar, a patisserie, a wood-burning pizza oven, a tandoor, a pro-digious tapas menu, a barbecue, a full-time oyster-shucker, a sommelier, and . . .

'Wahey!' said Julian. 'Sashimi! One nil!'

'So unfair,' said Dick. 'Bit early to eat though, isn't it?'

Julian was looking along the list of special menus for different days. 'Curry Thursday sounds good,' he said. '*And* Mexican Monday.'

'I think Weight Watcher's Wednesday has your name on it,' said Anne, patting his stomach.

By now George was quite recovered from her shock. Realising that Quentin was most likely not suffering from a health emergency, but had gone AWOL either through stupidity or by design, she was starting to get cross. And, having broken the seal, George discovered that she was angry with her father not simply for going missing in the garden centre, but for many other things besides.

'He never admits when I've done anything good,' she said grumpily.

'It certainly seems that he doesn't really listen if it's a girl talking,' admitted Anne.

'It goes deeper than that. If it's a female presenter on the telly, he either turns it over, or he just sits there and sniffs and tuts, or even laughs – until it's impossible to watch with him.'

'Well, he's a top-level scientist,' said Julian. 'Maybe he looks down on everyone.'

'But he's not,' said George. 'Top level, I mean. Not really. In terms of qualifications, at least. He got a low

2–2 from Cardiff University – that's it. The best you could say is that he's a very talented amateur.'

The others mulled this over, but George wasn't finished.

'I mean, I got a double first from Brighton,' she said. 'Then did a master's at Cambridge. For which I received a distinction. But he never once said well done.'

'He didn't say *anything*?' asked Dick.

George shook her head. She could see in Dick's eyes that he didn't quite believe that this was possible. She could see he thought Quentin must have said something or other, but that perhaps he had done so shyly, and that George hadn't quite caught it. With a bursting feeling of injustice, she was suddenly desperate to convince him.

'He fundamentally doesn't believe that, when a woman gets a qualification, it means the same as it does for a man,' she explained. 'I mean it. He thinks we get different, easier exams. And when you try to talk to him about it, he just switches off.'

'And he never praised you for your sporting achieve-ments,' Anne prompted her. 'Don't forget that.'

'Sporting achievements?' Dick asked. 'You, George?'

'So, have you always had trouble in your family relationships, then?' he asked sympathetically.

'Oh, Dick, did you have your head under a rock when we were at university?' Anne asked.

'Well, I was ... studying hard,' said Dick, catching Julian's eye. With a minute inclination of the head, Julian indicated Dick's secret was safe with him.

'You don't know about them because I don't bang on about them endlessly,' George said. 'Because I am not a bloke. I represented the university in judo, three years running. We got to the national finals each year. We even went to championships in Sweden, Brazil and San Francisco – I've got a handful of medals somewhere.'

'And you would have been part of the British Olympic archery team,' said Anne, 'if you hadn't got glandular fever. Tell them that.'

George nodded, while Dick looked at them both agape. He had always loved and respected his cousin, but he hadn't realized before now that she was a certified badass ...

'Daddy never came to a single competition or awards ceremony,' she said. 'And he never mentioned it. Even when Mummy did, he just changed the subject. And yet the football boots he wore when he had a try-out – a *try-out*, mind you – for Queens Park Rangers Under-18s get pride of place on the wall above the mantelpiece. And heaven help you if you so much as goes near *those* with a duster . . .'

Listening to this, Julian was getting increasingly hot under the collar. To think that all these years he had nurtured a desire to be liked and respected by Uncle Quentin. When, in fact, he was just a bloody misogynist right out of the old school. That I should have clasped such a viper, he thought, to my very bosom . . . Or, at least, given it votive offerings of port . . .

'But I didn't think there were any men like that anymore,' Julian said, aghast.

Anne just sighed.

'That's because you're not a woman,' George said. 'They're everywhere, mate.'

'Everywhere?' said Dick. 'Really?'

'Everywhere,' said George. 'Wherever we go, there they are. It's all day, every day. It never stops and it never will.'

'Is that true, Anne?' Dick asked.

Anne showed a very uncharacteristic flash of anger. 'Oh, of *course* it is,' she said. 'Why would George make it up?'

'But you've never said this to us,' said Dick. 'Why have you never made a fuss about it?'

'Well, it seems to be part of my nature, doesn't it, not making a fuss,' Anne said, frustrated. 'I never seem to make a fuss about anything. Except being bloody tidy. So I'm stuck with it.'

If Julian hated anything on this earth, it was a bully. Having always thought he was pretty much up to speed on the nature and prevalence of sexism, he was devastated to discover it was a thousand times more pervasive and continuous than he had suspected. He was even more dismayed by the fact that the population of bullies he had now to counteract constituted just under half the entire human race – and, very possibly, himself.

'Well, I'm glad you've told us,' he said. 'I'm going to give that rotter the ticking off of his life when we find him.'

'Yes,' said George. 'This is all about you, after all.'

'Just like a man,' Anne said.

CHAPTER EIGHT

The Gate to Paradise

Quentin seemed to have left the rest of the human race behind. He had wandered through the water-feature section, with its naked nymphs and trickling streams, and then drifted into a zone where he walked between stands of bamboo and delicately beautiful saplings.

For some reason, over the course of the last half hour or so, he hadn't bumped into anyone at all. Perhaps that was because it was Tuesday lunchtime, and the garden centre was always quiet around now. But it created an air that was half peaceful and half eerie. In fact, as he found himself walking among the full-grown fir trees (who bought these, and how did they get them home, he wondered?), Uncle Quentin had the feeling almost of being in Narnia . . .

Then he saw it, ahead of him. A small wooden gate in a narrow gap between two trees, incredibly easy to miss. It was rather picturesque, the sort of gate one would expect to lead to a pretty country cottage. On the gate was a small sign, written in flowing italic hand, which said, *The Gateway to Paradise.*

There was such an air of ethereal peace all around that Uncle Quentin experienced a moment's fear. Where was everyone? He glanced behind him, and then again at the gate, and its inscription.

He felt a pain in his chest and his hand clutched at it once more.

'Buggering phone,' he muttered. 'Why do I keep putting it back in that top pocket?'

He saw it was Anne calling, and let it go to voicemail. Then he stuffed it in his trouser pocket.

He moved forward, pushing open the gate. On the other side, steps fashioned from railway sleepers led steeply upwards. At the hill's crest, a few hundred yards away, a building was silhouetted against the sky. Smoke gently chugged from the chimney and even at this distance Uncle Quentin could identify the building's purpose from the sign that hung creaking in the wind.

*

It was dark inside, and thus impossible to see in through the frosted glass (which promised, in gold filigree, *Cask Ales, Fine Wines, Beers & Spirits – Good Food*). So, having paused to get his breath back after the climb, and to look at the pleasant fields hereabout, Quentin tested the handle. It gave easily, with a metal whine.

Once inside, his eyes adapting, Quentin understood why the legend upon the wooden gate had promised 'paradise'. On first inspection, he felt it was probably justified.

The pub was quiet, and old fashioned. Quentin found himself in a thickly carpeted saloon bar, with light streaming in through the windows, showing glamorous tumbling currents of dust. There were little touches that effortlessly won his approval – the bootscraper, the varnished Edwardian coat stand, and the King Charles Spaniel that lay on the carpet by the fire, tongue lolling.

The landlord was in the process of serving a pint of rich, golden ale to an elderly customer. As the landlord held it up it caught the light and the liquid took on the appearance of ambrosial nectar. They both paused to admire its beauty.

Quentin saw there were plenty of customers dotted

'Looking for a shed?' he asked.
'After a fashion,' said George. 'We're looking for a
bloke, and we think he's probably in one of them.'

around the room. Some were doing jigsaw puzzles at the oak tables, others reading mysteries and keeping to themselves in the leather armchairs. In one corner, there were pairs of chaps huddled around games of dominoes and cribbage.

There was a blazing fire in the grate and, next to it, a kindly, intelligent-looking chap, who paused in the middle of taking a sip of port, and looked over at Quentin.

'Close that bloody door, you oaf,' he said.

'Oh – of course,' said Quentin, shuffling inside.

He stood at the bar, where the landlord fetched him a pint of pale ale and a packet of pork scratchings.

It was blessedly *quiet*, Quentin thought. That was what made it so heavenly. He could see through into the public bar, where two old codgers were playing darts. Behind them, a television was showing the afternoon's racing, but with the sound turned down. Not far away was a bar billiards table. Nowhere in the entire building could be heard a single note of pop music.

Quentin settled at a chair by the bar, in order to peruse the available newspapers.

'Quite a place, this,' he said, seeing that each of the

beers on offer were among his favourites, and noting with approval that all the brass fittings were burnished to a cheerful shine.

'Yes,' said the landlord. 'Lots of my regulars seem to enjoy it. It's a little hideaway . . .'

'I'll say,' said Quentin. 'I don't want to leave.'

The landlord smiled. 'Well. You're welcome to stay until chucking-out time, at least.'

Quentin took his pint to peruse some of the books on the shelf by the door. They included a number that he had long intended to look into, and at length he selected Kingsley Amis's *On Drink*, tucking it under one arm and going to sit at a table. But soon enough Quentin got talking to his neighbour, and, soon after that, he was able to satisfy his curiosity about this place.

'Well, you see,' said his new friend, 'this pub was originally part of the nearby village. But we are all exiles from the garden centre, here. They know how to look after us, in this place,' he said, with satisfaction.

'They certainly do,' said Quentin, with feeling. He had picked up the laminated menu and was poring over it. The phone in his pocket buzzed, and he took it out. It was Anne again. He pocketed it.

'So, when you, er . . . escape,' Quentin said, trying to get past the word with the minimum of guilt, 'how long does it take for them to stop trying to contact you? Isn't it pretty much a constant?'

'Oh, an hour, maybe two,' said the other man. 'No more than that . . .'

'I think I'll have the gammon, egg and chips,' said Quentin, looking up from the menu.

CHAPTER NINE

Surveillance Culture

As they sat drinking wine, the four housemates shared stories of Quentin's grumpiness, unfriendliness and lackadaisical parenthood. Their irritation with him grew until they were found themselves possessed by an energetic desire to hunt him down.

They made their way to the front desk (Timmy trotting innocently behind), where they requested a message be broadcast to the entire complex. The woman on reception obliged at once, asking in an announcement if there was a Mr Kirrin, could he go to the front desk at once.

They waited.

'Here, little feller,' said the receptionist, who fell in love with Timmy at first sight. 'Have a treat.'

'That's not gluten-free, I suppose?' asked Dick.

'Oh yes,' she said. 'We sell them here.'

'TWO-nil!' shouted Julian, punching the air.

'And not a pony gas-mask to be seen,' said Dick, despondently.

'The trouble with this plan,' Julian said, after they had been waiting for half an hour, 'is that even if he heard the announcement, and he wanted to find the front desk, and he knew *where it was* – which I'm certain he doesn't – it would *still* take him about twenty minutes to get here. Professional cartographers could get lost in this place.'

'Tell me,' said the receptionist, 'does your father have any problems with his hearing?'

'Not that I know of . . .' said George. But that got her thinking again. Perhaps it would explain the frequent blank spells that came over Quentin, and his occasional inability to listen. Perhaps it wasn't selfishness or abstraction at all. And he was exactly the sort of man who would be too embarrassed to say something to his doctor. 'It's not impossible,' she admitted.

'Hmm,' said the receptionist. 'Well, there are some areas that aren't covered by the tannoy system. There's a good chance he just didn't hear it. It might be sensible to go and look at the CCTV.'

'There's CCTV here as well?' gasped Julian. 'Lordy, it's bloody everywhere!'

'We turn over three million pounds a week,' the receptionist said patiently. 'So imagine how much stock we have to keep at any one time. Not having that looked after by CCTV would be commercial suicide.'

'Hmm,' said Julian.

The receptionist, delighted to have these people off her hands, briskly delivered them to a security guard overseeing the bank of TV screens. This was a short, rather stocky woman with a buzz cut and a sharp, intense gaze, which (when it wasn't directed at the screens) had a tendency to drift towards George. Her badge introduced her with the words, *Hi! My name is* . . . This was followed by a biro squiggle and then a printed exclamation mark.

'Describe your uncle to me,' the squiggle-named woman said, after she had been apprised of the situation.

'He's perhaps a little overweight,' said Julian.

'Mid-sixties,' said George. 'Average height.'

'Not very smart clothes,' said Dick. 'Plenty of brown and beige . . .'

'Wears glasses,' said Anne.

74

'Where the blithering bloody heck have you been?'
George yelled.
'Well, I—' Quentin began.

The woman had been searching among the greyscale images on the screens, but now she turned to look at them.

'You just described about seventy per cent of our customers,' she said.

'Did we?'

'Well, look,' she said. 'Could any of these men be your father?'

She pointed at the screen directly in front of her. It showed the customers shambling around the pond displays. George groaned with dismay as she saw there were four men on this screen alone who could have been Quentin.

She turned to look at all the other screens. They were everywhere, these simulacra of her father, teeming like ants.

'It's impossible,' she said. 'We'll never find him.'

'Nonsense,' Anne said. 'We just watch the screens, and we ring him.'

'But he never picks up his phone,' said Dick.

'That doesn't matter – he might not answer it, but I bet he'll look at it, to make sure it's not an emergency, or someone phoning who he *does* want to talk to.'

The others nodded at this wisdom. It was a plan.

They took one corner of the bank of screens each, and studied hard, as Anne made the call.

The tense silence in the control booth was broken only by soft burr of the ringtone as Anne's phone connected. It buzzed once, twice, three times, and then they heard Quentin's voice.

The others looked at Anne expectantly. But she shook her head.

'Quentin here, leave message now,' said the voice at the other end.

'Well?' Anne asked. 'Did we see anything?'

Everyone shook their heads. Not a single person on the screen had so much as reached into their pocket, let alone looked at a device.

'How much of Garden Universe is covered by these cameras?' George asked.

'Whole place,' said the guard flatly. 'Every square inch.'

'That was a very clever idea of yours, Anne,' said Julian.

'Shame it didn't work,' Anne said.

'So, wait. He's . . . actually not here?' asked Dick.

'When I find that old git,' said George, 'I'm going to wring his bloody neck.'

CHAPTER TEN

Trouble in Paradise

Quentin was feeling very relaxed indeed. He'd had a proper pub lunch and several pints of beer, and was starting to feel that this was the most civilized afternoon he had spent for as long as he could remember.

After eating their lunch, several of the other patrons were feeling the same way, so where, formerly, gentle quietude had reigned, there was now a companionable loquacity.

'I've been coming here nine years,' said a gentleman in his seventies, with rather a drinker's nose, as he patted crisp crumbs off his cardigan. 'It's a dream come true.'

'This is my third year,' said another, more rustic type, in a woolly jumper and flat cap, with a walking stick hanging off the back of his chair. 'A home from home.'

'Better than home,' said another.

'Much better, seems to me,' said Quentin. 'No inter-ruptions, no fussing.'

'Hey,' said the landlord. 'We won't have that sort of language in here.'

Quentin put his hands up in apology. He had already been told there was to be no use of the 'F' word. Any derivative of 'fuss' was strictly prohibited.

'But I don't quite understand,' said Quentin. 'Surely you aren't left here *every* day? Why would your relatives keep bringing you?'

'No, no,' said the rustic type, laughing. 'We just dodged them that once, when we were first brought here. But, in doing so, we discovered this place. And saw it was for us. So we keep coming back.'

'I'm no stickler for the rules myself,' Quentin observed, 'but, ah, they frown quite heavily on drinking and driving these days, I hear . . .'

'Oh, no,' said the landlord, who was leaning on the bar with his chin resting on one hand, and listening in. 'There's none of that. Terry, out there, in the public bar, had to give up booze a few years back when he had trouble with his liver. He runs a minivan back and forth for a bunch of the regulars each day. For a consideration, of course. And the local taxi service does a good trade with us.'

'Hmm,' said Quentin. 'Oh, yes. Go on, then – I will have another, thank you, Ted. But tell me . . .' He was feeling dissatisfied on some sort of point, but it was hard to penetrate the woozy fog of contentment and remember what it was. 'Don't your relations, your wives and daughters and such, don't they . . . get their own back on you?'

'Oh, relations,' said Ted as he returned from the bar. Ted was a retired school teacher who had been a football referee in his spare time and liked to save up and go on cruises. They had only met forty minutes ago, but were already starting to feel like old friends. 'Relations, yes,' Ted repeated. 'Well,' he said. 'You know, I was never a particularly good father. I just never had the parenting knack. My wife was much better at that sort of thing.'

The farmer and the cardiganed man both nodded in agreement.

'I just don't think I had it in me,' said Ted. 'Naturally, they got fed up when I started disappearing up here, but . . . they eventually got the message. I mean, I miss them like the dickens. But they don't really speak to me anymore."

'Me too, me too,' said Mr Cardigan, whose name was, in fact, Arthur. 'It's very sad, but it's best this way. Rather than me just pretending to be what I'm not. I'm a rotten dad and grandad, you see? But I've come to terms with it.'

Beholding this semi-stranger, as he threw up his hands in a gesture of helpless innocence, a curiously unpleasant feeling stole over Quentin. The little speech this man had just delivered was one which, up until the moment he heard it from the lips of another, Quentin might very well have made himself. But being its recipient was vividly appalling to him. It was patently evident that this man had never tried to be a good father – or any kind of father, even. The ease with which he gave up this unique privilege and responsibility was hideous. It was smug, pathetic and cowardly. To conceal his horror, Uncle Quentin scooped up his pint of Truman and took a deep draught in three long gulps.

Setting his drink back down, he sought to change the conversation. He didn't want to provoke these new friends, after all.

'Darling,' Quentin said.
'Don't "darling" me,' George shouted. 'What have you
been doing? Where were you?'

'So, have you always had trouble in your family relationships, then?' he asked sympathetically. He envisioned tales of broken marriages, drugs and delinquency.

'Oh, no, not a bit of it,' said Arthur, digging into his wallet. 'Look, here; this is my Becky. Isn't she beautiful? First of my family to go to university. Went to Bournemouth. Now she works in retail in Hemel Hempstead.' He beamed with pride while saying this, in seeming contradiction of the meaning of his words. 'Twenty-nine. Isn't she beautiful?'

Quentin looked down his nose at Becky's photograph. It seemed to him that, in a beauty contest between herself and a walrus that had recently been in a bar fight, Becky would come second. But he kept this thought to himself, and merely nodded.

'This is my Stephanie,' said the farmer, holding out another photo. 'Wonderful girl. Got two of her own little ones now. They must be . . . oh, three and five. Her husband's an estate agent in Colchester. They've got a nice semi-detached, which he brokered himself.'

Quentin nodded again, smiled diffidently, and handed the photo back.

He felt a gorgeous swell of pride as the words he was about to say rose to his lips. 'Pfff,' he wanted to utter. 'They're nothing. You should see my George. First from Brighton, master's from Cambridge. Near as dammit represented Britain at the London Olympics!'

But, in the very act of beginning to say it, he realized how much he disgusted himself. What, he thought, am I doing here, about to boast of my daughter's achievements to these lazy old gits, when I've never even spoken to George about them? These men gave up their daughters long ago. But mine's right here, only a few hundred yards away.

'Tell me,' Quentin said, on a whim. 'Did you ever tell them that you loved them? Or give them encouragement?'

'I wasn't brought up that way,' said Ted stoically. 'That wasn't how we did things.'

'I wouldn't know how to start,' said Arthur. 'It's not really in my . . .' he squirmed. 'You know, in my vocabulary.'

'Mine neither,' said the farmer.

'Didn't you at least *try*—?' Quentin was about to ask. But, as though this talk of emotions had disturbed the equilibrium of the place, he was cut off at once.

84

'Nearly time for the afternoon quiz,' said Ted loudly, folding his newspaper and resettling his glasses on his nose. 'Where's my pencil? Ah. Not joining us, Quentin?'

'No, sorry,' said Quentin, downing his remaining beer. 'I've suddenly remembered I've got to be somewhere.'

He was filled with a fearful urgency. There was only one thing he had come to this garden centre to get, and he hadn't done it. He just hoped he would be in time, before George gave up and drove home, leaving him here . . .

CHAPTER ELEVEN

El Mundo del Sheddo

George, Julian, Dick and Anne stared gloomily at the CCTV screens, then one by one they turned to go, Julian stroking Timmy's head as he followed them out.

'Wait,' said the security guard. 'I forgot. There's one area that isn't covered by our cameras. Apart from the Charlie Dimmock Café, of course – but that's closed for renovations. It's Shed World – right at the back of the lot, extending up the hill. Part of Garden Universe, but a separate company – they have their own security systems. You could try there.'

'Of course!' said Anne. 'That's what we came for, after all!'

'I'll bet he's there,' said George, scrunching her fists menacingly.

'To the shediverse!' cried Julian.

'Woof!' said Timmy.

'You really have to get that dog out of here,' said the security guard.

It was a long ten-minute walk from the security guard's sanctuary to the very far end of the garden centre, where Shed World resided. They would have reached it in good time had they not lost Julian on the way. After a brief search, they discovered him back at the wine terrace.

'I thought it would be safest to retreat to a place we all knew, and wait for you to find me,' he said, between quick swigs of a large glass of pinot, 'rather than us all charging round the place and missing each other for hours on end.'

Anne opened her mouth to castigate him, but George abbreviated the process by giving him a cuff round the ear, after which they were off again.

Soon they were passing beneath a large arch, which proclaimed itself the entrance to Shed World. The arch was so vast it could easily have served as the entryway into some exotic theme park, and the effect of walking underneath, and into a giant space filled with vacant wooden buildings, was somewhat unnerving.

Built up on the hill, as they were, the sheds seemed

to loom somewhat massively above them, and gather, in the early evening gloom, into a strange and sinister mass. Their animal companion did not share their reservations. He seemed to get a scent at once and hared off between two huts. They heard a bark or two afterwards, but they were content to let him explore on his own, for the time being.

'Hello!' said a friendly voice, making them jump. They looked up. A placid man in his fifties, wearing stone-washed jeans, a navy linen jacket and with a pencil-thin beard traced along his jawline, was looking down at them from the staircase to a hut that stood on stilts. Unlike all the other sheds in sight, this one had lights blazing from its windows.

'Looking for a shed?' he asked.

'After a fashion,' said George. 'We're looking for a bloke, and we think he's probably in one of them.'

He beckoned them to join him, as he retreated into his office.

'We like to think we cater to every taste, here, at Shed World,' said the man, sitting in the chair behind his desk, leaning back and regarding them through his glasses. 'My name is Martyn. Tea?'

'Martyn T. what?' asked Julian.

'No, thanks,' said George. 'We just want to find my father.'

'A shed for every type of man,' said Martyn. 'Or woman,' he corrected himself. Then he burst out laughing. 'Oh, sorry. That's just a little joke we have in the shed trade. No, seriously, for every type of man, there is a type of shed. And I like to think we cater to more people than any other shed emporium in the northern hemisphere. Coffee?'

'No, thanks,' said Dick. 'You mean there's a bigger one in the southern hemisphere?'

Martyn's easy affability vanished. His eyes flashed to a picture on the wall, and everyone followed his gaze. There, they saw the picture of a man who looked exactly like Martyn, except he was adorned by a flamboyant moustache, a poncho and a jazzy smile. On the frame was written, *El Mundo del Sheddo – La Paz*.

'Oh, I'll get you one day, Martinez,' he said under his breath, in a ragged whisper.

Then, at once, he was all friendliness again.

'As I say,' he said, 'the widest selection of sheds in the northern – and, I like to say, *best*ern – hemisphere. Let me tell you about a few of them, see which one we think your father would have been drawn to. Bovril? Horlicks?'

They shook their heads.

'I assure you, we are adequately refreshed,' said George. 'Now, hit me,' she added. 'Shedwise.'

'The sauna shed,' Martyn said.

'No, no.'

'Hot-tub paradise shed.'

'No.'

'The retirement boudoir. Like a conservatory, just not attached to the house.'

'No. Keep them coming; I'll stop you.'

'The video-game den. The Japanese tea room. The sex dungeon.'

'It's my *dad* you're talking about.'

Martyn spread out his hands. 'It's also lots of my customers,' he said. 'Okay, I'll keep going. The survivalist bunker . . .'

'Hmmm,' George said. 'Nnnno . . .'

'To buy a shed,' *she yelled. 'That's what we came for!'*

'The sports pavilion.'

'Nope!'

'It's great, that one – comes with dartboard, full-sized snooker table.'

'I don't want your life story, mate,' George said. 'Keep coming with the sheds.'

'Pirate castle,' said Martyn. 'Then there's a bouncy shed. But those are both for children, really. Or the mentally ill. There's Ye Olde Shedde Pubbe?'

'No, no, he does his secret drinking in secret, like an Englishman,' said George. 'You have to smell it on his breath. He wouldn't want to advertise the thing. Have you got anything like, er, a . . . laboratory?'

'Oh, yes, indeed,' said Martyn. 'You should have said. I'll take you to it at once. I assume, if we find the right shed for your father, there's a sale in it?'

'Oh, yes, indeed,' mimicked Julian. 'But no findo Quentin, no sello shed.' And he tapped his wrist where a watch would go. 'Tick tock.'

'Sorry,' said Anne. 'He's pissed.'

'Who isn't?' asked Martyn.

'Tick tock' proved to be an unfortunately prophetic phrase. Martyn took them along to the laboratory hut, but at first sight they could all tell it was far too primitive for Quentin's purposes. It might just about pass muster for a rank amateur, a beginner equipped with a schoolboy's chemistry set. But George knew her father would find it beneath his contempt.

'Where's the centrifuge?' she asked.

Martyn looked over her shoulder. 'I think it's just past Salisbury on the A361,' he said.

'You can't have a lab without a centrifuge,' George insisted. 'Even I know that. No, no, no.'

'Well, I'm afraid that's the only one of its sort that we have,' said Martyn. 'And, if you want to see more sheds, I must ask you to come back tomorrow. This is just about our closing time . . .'

George and Anne looked at each other, aghast.

'But this is *awful*,' said George. 'I can't just leave Daddy here.'

'He's gone to ground,' said Julian. 'He is *in* hiding. That's worse than ordinary hiding.'

As they spoke, they walked along with Martyn, who

trotted out beneath the arch, pulled the gates of Shed World closed behind him, locked it with a padlock and disappeared into the encroaching shadows with a cheery wave.

They stood there, for once utterly flummoxed.

'Woof,' said Timmy doubtfully.

'Woof, indeed,' said Julian. 'You hit the nail on the bloody head, mate.'

'What do we do now?' asked Anne. 'We've looked everywhere and he's not *any*where. This was the one place we knew he wanted to go. He's vanished!'

George was looking distraught.

'Well,' she said at last, 'I suppose . . . we go home. Leave him here. Perhaps that's what he really wants.'

The others didn't want to admit this was true. But, reluctantly, they now had to acknowledge that it might be. They felt for George, but she was oblivious to their sympathetic stares. Having made up her mind, she was marching ahead of them, towards the exit.

'Come on,' she said. 'They're closing shortly. We don't want to get locked in.'

Then, as they turned a corner past the tropical

greenhouse, a familiar silhouette emerged from the dusk. They all stopped.

'Oh,' said Quentin.

Even in the failing light, none of them could mistake his shock at seeing them – or miss the rictus of shame and embarrassment that took hold of his expression. No teenager caught in an act of petty rebellion had ever looked so guilty.

'Oh,' he said again.

George took a deep breath.

CHAPTER TWELVE

Trial and Retribution

'Where the blithering bloody heck have *you* been?' George yelled.

'Well, I—' Quentin began.

'Have you got any idea how worried I was?' she asked.

'Woof,' Timmy agreed, heartily.

The others had been afraid of witnessing this confrontation, and of feeling horrendously awkward. But now it had come, they were all so heartily on George's side that they found themselves eager for vengeance, and for Quentin to account for himself.

'Darling,' Quentin said.

'Don't "*darling*" me!' George shouted. 'What have you been doing? Where were you?'

Quentin hesitated. Quite often, he had found throughout his adult life, when you hesitated, someone (like friendly Anne) stepped in to fill the silence. Not now, though.

They all waited for him to speak. None of them actually tapped their feet, but there was a distinctly foot-tapping aspect to the silence.

'I just wandered off,' he said.

'Why?' George asked.

Quentin hesitated again, and once again it aided him not one jot. He became flustered.

'I just fancied some time alone,' he said.

'*Why*?' George asked.

Quentin was now really thoroughly on the spot. He hadn't felt so bowel-looseningly humiliated since public school, more than fifty years ago. He was in fact so thoroughly rattled and resourceless that he appeared close to tears. Seeing this, his nephews and niece at last began to feel sorry for him.

'It was very selfish. I'm sorry,' he said quietly. 'I do realize ... I know you think I don't, but I do ... I *do* see ... how selfish I've been.'

'Can you imagine what went through my head?' George asked. 'I thought I'd find you lying somewhere, dead or comatose. Or being wheeled into an ambulance!'

'I didn't think of that,' admitted Quentin.

'Of course not. You just take me for granted. And then the inconvenience. Julian, Dick and Anne all agreed to come today because it sounded like a nice day out for us all – together. But instead we've spent hours and hours chasing around after you.'

'Woof,' Timmy agreed again.

'I really *am* sorry,' said Quentin, and now there was a tremble in his voice that made both Anne and Dick feel their hearts might cave in.

'I think he is genuinely sorry, George, as he says,' Dick said.

'Please, George,' said Anne. 'The garden centre's closing. Perhaps we could talk this through later.' Although she did not at all relish the long ride back to south Dorset.

George sighed, and looked at the floor.

'I think we should shoot the bugger,' said Julian.

This at least startled George out of her reverie. The first energy of her fury was spent, but there remained much she was still angry about.

'Who's going to bring you back here, Daddy?' she asked. 'Did you think about that?'

'Back?' he asked. 'What for?'

'*To buy a shed*,' she yelled, up at the early evening stars. 'That's what we came for!'

'Oh, no – I bought a shed weeks ago,' he said.

If Quentin had expected this revelation to thaw his audience's feelings, he was mistaken. There was a new frostiness as Julian asked, 'What?'

'All the sheds are available online. They had a sale on, in fact. Saved myself three hundred quid.' He smiled at them.

Julian had only been joking, of course, when he mentioned shooting his uncle. But suddenly the prospect of assassination lurched closer to reality.

Dick cleared his throat. 'So what are we doing here, Uncle?' he asked.

'And what's that bloody thing in your arms? A Venus flytrap?' George said.

'It's the reason I knew I had to come here,' Quentin said, looking down at it. 'It's a special plant. Incredibly valuable, and unbelievably rare. Hardly any have ever been raised in captivity, outside of its native land.'

The four didn't know quite what to make of this. Fortified by their silence, Quentin continued.

'I could never find a better way of telling you the way
I saw you . . . than by giving you this.'

'Do you remember, darling—?' Quentin began.

'I've warned you about using the "D" word, Daddy,' George said.

'Let him finish, George,' said Anne, 'or we'll never get out of here.'

'I told you about my excursions into the jungles of Borneo, thirty years ago, didn't I?' Quentin persisted.

'When you nearly had your arm bitten off by a tiger?'

'It wasn't a tiger, I've told you this before. It was a type of big cat native to the jungles that hug the northern coast. They have these stripes . . .'

'Bloody Nora!' said Julian. 'Now you're *both* getting off the point! Come on, let's walk and talk. Otherwise we'll be stuck here overnight. The main building's this way. Uncle, please get on with the story.'

'Oh, yes,' said Quentin, as they all started walking alongside each other.

It was strangely difficult to remain antagonistic towards someone walking by your side, George discovered, and she tried to fight back the natural sense of gladness and relief she felt at having Quentin back.

'Well,' he went on, 'after an arduous trek into the heart

of the jungle, I discovered a plant, which – as I said – is extremely rare. It is incredibly hardy, surviving in any environment. But it blooms exceptionally rarely. Even among the local tribespeople, very few had ever seen it flower. But I did.'

'Right,' said George, not really listening. The main building was in sight, now, and she was hunting in her pocket for the car key.

'Because it blooms so rarely, it's cultivated practically nowhere. But I happened to know that a seed from the original plant we brought back had been planted in the tropical house here. Then, just a few days ago, I heard it had come into bloom. The only one that has flowered in Europe, in the last thirty years.'

The four housemates leant forward to peer at the plant in Quentin's arms, in the meagre light.

The plant itself was nothing special. Its outer leaves were more or less rusks, looking like dried reeds. Quentin touched these outer fronds.

'It's coated in these for most of its life. They form a very hard shell, almost impossible to penetrate by any bird or insect – even in the jungle.'

But the flower was beautiful. There were several layers of elegantly curling petals, in shades that were hard to make out in the dusk, but which seemed to hint, from the bottom up, at rosy pink, rich orange and gold. Each petal came to a sharp point, which was tipped with startling scarlet.

Looking upon this flower, all were struck by its extra-ordinary beauty and complexity. All except Timmy, who couldn't see, and kept jumping up and throwing his fore-legs on George's arms.

'Woof,' Timmy said.

'Shut up for a second,' George said to him. 'What did you call it?' she asked Quentin.

'Well,' Quentin said, 'you were only very little then. But already I could see that you took after me, in having a rough exterior. Yet,' he said quietly, and somewhat diffidently, for he had never spoken to his daughter (or anyone) this intimately before, 'I could see that you were so much more – so beautiful and complicated – and that I could never find a better way of telling you the way I saw you . . . than by giving you this.'

He handed the pot to her.

'George, meet *Georgia georgiae*,' he said quietly.

She took the pot from him, her hands trembling. She couldn't take her eyes off the flower. Partly because she didn't trust her eyes – which had been brimming for what seemed like ages – not to begin flowing.

'It's beautiful,' she said.

'*She's* beautiful, you mean,' said Quentin.

There were many issues between father and daughter left unconquered in this short conversation. But, in this moment, all those other things were briefly overwhelmed by this extraordinary gift: this singular way her uncommunicative father had found to articulate his feelings for his daughter.

Rather than ruin the beautiful silence between them, George slipped her arm into his, and walked with her father to the exit.

At last, they could leave Garden Universe, relieved of some of the burdens with which they had entered.

'I suppose, I sort of . . .' she said. 'You know what I'm trying to say.'

'No need to say it,' Quentin said. 'You know how I feel about the "L" word.'

She nodded. 'Well. I do, anyway.'

'Yes,' Quentin said, squeezing her arm. 'Me too.'

'I'll treasure this always,' George said, looking at the flower once again, as they went out into the car park. She stood on tiptoes and kissed Quentin on the cheek.

'Good,' he said.

They walked on for a few strides in quiet contentment.

'Don't tell your mother,' he muttered into her ear. 'But it was fucking expensive.'

George laughed so loud that Timmy jumped.

'Woof!' he protested. He ran around Quentin and George in circles, wagging his tail furiously, as father gave daughter a loving kiss. But it wasn't only George's contentment he was celebrating. In all the confusion, the project to replace his basket (which he had been wise to from the start) had been forgotten entirely. At least there was one old dog who would not be forced to learn new tricks.

'Woof!' he barked, in celebration. 'Woof, woof!'